MW01103414

PASS THE PROMOTION,
PLEASE

Lewena Bayer and Karen Mallett

GREAT PLAINS
PUBLICATIONS

Great Plains Publications
3 - 161 Stafford Street
Winnipeg, MB R3M 2W9
www.greatplains.mb.ca

Great Plains Publications gratefully acknowledges the financial support
provided for its publishing program by the Government of Canada
through the Book Publishing Industry Development Program (BPIDP).

Design & Typography by Gallant Design
Printed in Canada by Kromar Printing Ltd.

CANADIAN CATALOGUING IN PUBLICATION DATA

Bayer, Lewena

Pass the promotion please

      (In good company ; 3)

      ISBN 1-894283-22-8

1.   Business etiquette.   2.   Business Communication
I. Mallett, Karen.

II. Title.   III. Series: Bayer, Lewena. In good company ; 3.

HF5389.B39 2001   395.5'2   C2001-910924-5

I'd like to give heart-felt thanks to Jill Morinello, Pamela Barton, Joyce Stokoe and Laurie Slater who through the years (it can't be that many, can it?) have supported me unconditionally, listened without comment and can still make me laugh until my sides hurt.

Karen

This book is dedicated to Florence Hicks, Cathy Shaver, Hazel Zaharik, Freda Reeve and Mariette Bayer. I thank them for the unconditional kindness, support and courtesy they have shown me over the years— at times when I needed it most. Each has had a significant and distinctive impact on my life.

Lewena

Table of Contents

INTRODUCTION:
What's in it for me?

"Etiquette is about respect and leadership, taking the time to put others at ease and thinking before you act."

—The Etiquette Ladies

Good manners are an investment in yourself and in your business. Business etiquette rules provide a blueprint for behavior in business situations. Most every workplace is different and the blueprint must be adjusted suitably. Some executives seemingly make it to the top without exercising good manners, nevertheless, as in the game of life, there are rules in business and if you don't know the rules, you'll be lucky to win the game. While people rarely comment on good manners when they see them, they certainly notice when courtesy is absent. Accordingly, you can be sure that good social skills and proper corporate conduct will give you a step up on the competition and ease your rise to the top of the corporate ladder.

Imagine this scenario. Three equally qualified employees are in competition for a major promotion within their company. All have formal university educations, extensive in-house training, and equivalent seniority. The interview process includes all the basic questions and skill testing. At the end of the day, the candidates are neck in neck. Because the chosen candidate will be representing the company in many social situations where business and pleasure will mix, the hiring committee administers another test. Each candidate is invited to attend a luncheon meeting with a potential client. Although all three candidates presented well in the interviewing process, it is their ability to convert their "professional" manners outside the office that will determine their ability to handle ANY business situation.

One candidate is quite obviously uncomfortable in this scenario. She gets straight to business instead of allowing time for small talk over the meal; remains somber throughout the luncheon as if pitching a hard deal in a boardroom; squirms, looks at her watch too often, and fails to maintain eye contact during non-business conversation; she lets negative comments slip out about the timeliness of the lunch service; and, finally, takes offense when the male client holds the door for her while they are leaving. She is all business and forgets that this is also a social situation. Many important, lasting relationships can be formed and much can be learned about a client in this kind of social setting—these relationships and this information can then be very useful in the boardroom.

Another candidate is all too comfortable at the luncheon. He shakes hands with the client forcibly and maintains physical contact for far too long; addresses the client by their first name in a very informal fashion; gives too much intimate personal information about himself; pats the client on the arm after laughing at his own jokes; and interrupts the client to call out to friends and associates seen across the restaurant. He forgets that this is not just a social situation but a business one as well! Overly familiar and casual behavior in a social/business setting makes the client uncomfortable and can cause them to run away instead of bringing them closer. Besides, the candidate revealed more about himself than the client did.

All of these behaviors may indicate to the interviewers that the applicants are nervous, but to the clients the candidates appear disinterested, not in control of the situation, overly familiar, negative, and basically, rude. The candidates surely don't mean to give a bad impression; but they surely won't get the promotion either.

The candidate who handles himself with grace and diplomacy, asks the right questions, appears relaxed but not overly so, conducts business informally when everyone is comfortable and ready to do so—this is the candidate who wins not only the promotion but the potential client as well!

As a leader in industry it is essential that you can be trusted to conduct yourself with decency and self-respect in any situation. When you know that you have the polish and social skills to handle anything, you will come across as confident, competent and at ease. Companies are realizing the added potential employees bring to the table when they have had training in corporate conduct. This knowledge puts you one step ahead of the competition and sends you on your way to that once elusive promotion in the sky.

Chapter One

STARTING AT THE SOURCE: Dealing with clients and customers

Many of us start our careers on the "front lines," dealing face to face with clients and the general public in entry-level jobs, or working in service-oriented professions while we prepare for our "real jobs." A lot of the lessons we learn in dealing with clients and customers are the same lessons that can further our careers when we start to move up the ranks in our chosen professions. How we handle ourselves in these front-line positions is a pretty good indicator of our attitude towards serving others. And, it is often this service attitude that predicts whether or not we will successfully apply these client management skills to our interpersonal relationships with difficult bosses or co-workers. This aptitude ultimately determines our employment futures.

Modern business etiquette is all about showing others care and consideration, maintaining our calm in the most chaotic situations, and handling every scenario with confidence and grace. Professionals in every type of business need to successfully navigate the "manners minefield" in their daily workplace. Daily interaction with higher-ups, peers and clients in particular, can be difficult at best. Knowing how to anticipate problems before they happen, dealing effectively with complicated issues and developing strong interpersonal relationships can help things run smoothly and productively. These are extremely important issues if you want to get noticed come promotion time. What's your service attitude? Take this self-assessment and find out.

Quiz: Self-assessment

	True or False
Answer true or false to each of the following:	
1. When dealing with clients, you should always make eye contact with women first.	
2. If you are almost finished your shift and don't really have time to deal with a client issue, you should ask the client to reschedule or come back later.	
3. When a client is angry about something that is clearly not your fault, tell them so, and then go ahead and call the manager over.	
4. Regardless of your position, it is more important to dress so that you are comfortable and stylish rather than to worry about what other people may think.	
5. When someone shows little emotion when speaking, it indicates that they care little about the issue at hand.	
6. When someone gives a lengthy explanation or seems to go into too much detail about something, you should interrupt them and ask for the "short and sweet" version.	
7. If a customer is yelling and visibly upset, it is best to take them somewhere more private to talk.	
8. Being a good listener is a big part of good customer service.	
9. If you tell someone you will do something, it is very important to actually have the power to do it.	
10. When it comes to customer service, most people don't care how long the solution takes, just as long as the issue is resolved eventually.	

(See answers at the end of this chapter.)

A. I didn't mean it, honest! Old habits are hard to break

When it comes to modern business, we've all developed bad habits. You could call it "unintentional rudeness." Customers and clients may be so accustomed to these less than courteous behaviors that they don't take offense at them. However, being a respectful adult and a professional requires that we lead by example and display high standards of behavior. Unfortunately, most of us have just gotten used to incivility and use the fact that we tolerate it from customers as an excuse to repeat it ourselves. Old habits are hard to break, but any way you look at it, unintentional rudeness is still rudeness!

Put yourself in the customer's shoes for a moment. Think of a time when you were not particularly impressed with the service you received. Maybe you experienced one of the following rude behaviors, which are often reported by clients.

- **Don't point your finger at me buddy!** It is extremely unprofessional for clients to be put in a position where they have to witness someone being criticized in public. This often happens when a higher up is not satisfied with an entry-level person's behavior or in training situations. If you're in charge, don't publicly criticize your employees. You never know who is listening or what their relationship is to the person with whom you may be speaking.

- **Play the role.** Believe it or not, customers recognize and remember improper business attire. You may be especially proud of your new belly button tattoo but customers will be uncomfortable when they can't help staring at it because of the midriff top you're wearing. It is extremely important that professionals and support staff both look and act the part of polished, competent and caring individuals. Make sure clothes or uniforms are neat, clean and fit properly. Keep hair and nails clean and well-groomed. Wear proper shoes and avoid excess perfume or makeup. Gum chewing is another bad habit that should be avoided.

■ **Be the keeper of the clock.** One of the rudest things service people can do is be disrespectful of other people's time. It is terribly rude to impose a lack of organization or control on others. Try to adopt good time management habits. Clients or interviewees who are on time should be acknowledged and where possible, they should be informed of long delays in advance. At the very least, personnel should apologize for delays. Certainly it is understandable that we all have complicated responsibilities and sometimes waiting time cannot be avoided, however, it is unreasonable to expect clients to wait long periods without explanation or apology.

■ **Avoid the ring of death.** Ask any customer and they will tell you that nothing gets them angrier faster than rude telephone behavior. If there's one thing that can kill your business quickly, it's telephone rudeness. This applies to being placed on hold for extended periods, voicemail instead of live voices, outdated telephone systems, incorrect call transfers, failure to identify oneself on the phone, curt tone of voice and failure to return calls. It's imperative that the telephone be handled properly, particularly if it will be the first contact your client has with your company.

■ **I can't get any respect.** The fact that a customer may wait in line quietly or smile when you input the wrong amount on their credit card for the second time does not mean that you should take their good nature for granted. It is very important to acknowledge polite behaviors. Acknowledge when a customer is on time, has completed paperwork appropriately, arrives at an appointment prepared, follows directions, or has been especially patient. Front line and support staff should make efforts to show appreciation by smiling and thanking clients.

- **Excuse me, please.** If you are in the midst of a face-to-face interaction with someone, show them the respect of giving them your full attention. This means avoiding inappropriate interruptions. Don't take other telephone calls or carry on more than one conversation at a time. If you are interrupted by someone or something, apologize for the interruption and immediately return to the client with whom you are dealing. Whenever possible, complete the task at hand and then move on to the next issue.

- **I swear...** Newsflash! Customers have ears. They can hear nearby conversations between employees and other clients and/or conversations that employees may be engaged in with each other. Often staff members forget that clients can hear their conversations and they will carry on, vulgar and inappropriate language included, as if no one is listening. In-house procedures, client files, internal/interpersonal issues and personal issues or problems should not be discussed except behind closed doors. Similarly, the type of language used and the emotions which are expressed should be carefully monitored. Swearing and foul language is offensive and reflects poorly on the company.

B. Give me a break already: Dealing with difficult people

Let's face it. Customer service is rarely easy! It's hard enough to worry about controlling your own behavior, never mind the behavior of others—especially when it seems like the person you're dealing with is from another planet. Some days, it seems like the whole world has gotten up on the wrong side of the bed. It doesn't help that we've all gotten so used to assuming the worst about people that we're automatically suspicious. Even if someone does or says something nice, we're often on the defensive before we even know if there is actually a problem. Here are some examples of potentially difficult client service situations that could arise. What would you do in each case?

Quiz: Office scenarios

1. Linda is juggling two phone lines and walk-in clients at the same time. In the midst of giving client information over the phone, a walk-in client approaches the desk. Hello, Mr. Impatient! Although it's obvious that Linda is otherwise engaged, Mr. Impatient paces in front or her desk with a disgruntled look on his face. Between glances at his watch he's sending her one of those "get off the darned phone" looks. What should Linda do?

2. Mr. Ima Somebody is a regular client. He is notorious for canceling, rescheduling and being late. When and if Mr. Somebody finally decides to show up, he is consistently rude to the front line staff and demands a lot of attention. The front-line people really dread seeing him. Is it appropriate to say something to him? If so, who should do it, the manager/boss or an administrative person?

3. A particular customer, let's call him Matthew Mascot, has appointed himself the company spokesperson. He has a habit of becoming engrossed in long conversations with other clients while they're waiting for scheduled meetings. He has been overheard giving "expert" advice and expressing some opinions about the company's service and products that are neither correct nor appropriate. His conversations are beginning to cause some concern with the employees who overhear them, and more and more clients are looking worried and asking strange questions. What should the front line person do?

4. You happen to walk into the conference room and observe a client, now referred to as Ten Fingers Tina, leafing through confidential files. You also notice some office supplies bulging out of her jacket pocket. What should you do?

5. Ricky Suave, a pretty slick customer indeed, has expressed a "personal interest" in your co-worker. As a result he's been asking personal questions, hanging around a lot and telephoning regularly to schedule unnecessary appointments. How should this situation be handled?

(Check at the end of the chapter for the etiquette ladies' suggestions on how to handle these scenarios.)

Obviously, there is an endless array of possibilities when it comes to humans and unpredictable behavior. In almost every situation, however, keeping your cool and lending an ear leads to a quick and relatively painless resolution. When things don't go as planned, take a deep breath and try again. You may think that when things get messy, the best solution is to call the manager. Save this as a last resort. Remember, how competently you handle the front line is a reflection on how ready you are to be removed from the front line. Your service attitude is showing and your reputation is at stake, so be careful not to be one of these not so successful customer service people.

MEGAPHONE MERV: If you have an embarrassing problem, do whatever you can to get a serviceperson other than Merv. He says whatever pops into his head and he says it loudly. If you were hoping to have the issue handled discretely and without causing a scene, you'd better leave your sunglasses on and use someone else's name.

I'll be with you in a minute. My nails are drying.

THE PRINCESS: This prim and perfect customer service person looks capable but she's far too busy preening herself in the mirror behind the angry customer to notice that he's getting madder by the minute. She'd like to help you lift the return box but heaven forbid she break a nail. Smiling would smear her lip gloss and she certainly doesn't want to break a sweat helping you—you never know when Prince Charming will come along.

How should you react when you come across customer service situations that seem unmanageable? Here are ten handy tips on dealing with the not so pleasant.

1. **Maintain your sense of humor.** It's amazing what a smile can accomplish.

2. **Stay calm.** If you get excited, so will the customer.

3. **Collect your thoughts.** If you stop to think about it, things are rarely as bad as they initially seem.

4. **Respond with manners.** Courtesy is reciprocal and people have a tendency to treat you the way you treat them.

5. **Leave if you must regain composure.** Try not to let anyone see you when you are unable to control your emotions.

6. **Lead by example.** Always be mindful of who may be listening or watching.

7. **Do not embarrass or humiliate.** It's far easier and far more effective to be nice.

8. **Remain positive.** If you haven't anything positive to say, say nothing or be neutral.

9. **Change the subject.** If someone brings up or persists in discussing an inappropriate topic, change the subject. This is one situation where interrupting may even be acceptable.

10. **Give the benefit of the doubt.** Don't make assumptions about the motives or attitudes of others. Make sure you have all the facts before you jump to conclusions.

C. Artful dodging: Avoiding conversation catastrophes

Have you ever found yourself forced to engage in a conversation with someone who simply does not communicate? You know, when getting more than a one-word response is like pulling teeth. Typically the "non-speaker" is either excruciatingly shy or they just don't understand that conversations involve two people taking turns asking questions and responding. How many times have you seen two people look at each other, smile uncomfortably and then look away because one of them simply has nothing to say beyond hello? The trick here is to encourage not to discourage. You can do this by asking leading questions that show interest and encourage a speaker to say more. One of the quickest and most effective ways to get someone to keep talking is to look at them wide-eyed and say "really"? Try it, you'll be amazed at what you might learn.

And what if you're seated next to Larry LockJaw at the next business luncheon? Try to find out what he's interested in. As soon as you get the first "yes" out of him, pounce on him with "Oh, I'd like to hear more about fly-fishing," or "Larry, please tell me more about your dog, Shep." You'll have to pay attention though and practise your wide-eyed, interested look to keep the Lockjaw from clamming up again.

Other leading questions or comments that work well include:

- Could you be more specific?

- Gee, that is fascinating!

- What an interesting…

- What do you think about…

D. Who's serving whom? The internal customer

When you're not out on the front lines, you don't have to worry about customer service anymore, right? Wrong. It's important to recognize that when it comes to business interactions, it's sometimes difficult to determine who is serving whom. Have you ever heard of an internal customer? Internal customers are everyone you work with. This includes your co-workers, higher-ups, suppliers, building managers—anyone who you may come in contact with during the course of your business day. It's especially important to recognize that every one of these people formulates an opinion about you, your service attitude, your professionalism and your competency. Every comment, every action, every problem is witnessed by others and these people will, in part, help to determine your success. Just as you want to sell your product to the external customers, you want and need to sell yourself to the internal customers.

E. Listen up!

We've all heard that the best conversationalist is a good listener, right? Oh, I'm sorry did you say something? Well, it is indeed true that one of the most respected but least practised polite behaviors is listening. Customers and co-workers alike would agree that problems could be solved more quickly and a lot more could be accomplished if people would just listen. What constitutes a good listener? Here are some tips:

■ **Be sincere!** If you are not really interested, or it is just not a good time, say so. Show others the respect of not wasting their time. If you do initiate a conversation or ask a question, focus on the speaker and make a sincere effort to listen to the response.

■ **Use your body.** Your body language should show interest. Make direct eye contact as you listen, and smile or nod if you agree with what is being said to encourage the speaker to go on. Don't fold your arms across your chest or fidget as both these behaviors can signal closed-mindedness.

■ **Ask away.** Ask intelligent, relevant questions. Don't pretend to understand something if you don't and don't let a speaker go on and on about something if you haven't the foggiest idea what they're trying to say. It's far more courteous to stop the speaker and ask for clarification than to let them go on.

■ **No interruptions, please**. Do not interrupt unless absolutely necessary. If you must interrupt—if you need clarification, for instance—make eye contact and state the speaker's name and then your reason for interrupting. Make the interruption brief and do not take over the speaker's role unless the interrupted speaker indicates it's appropriate to do so. Keep in mind that inappropriate interruptions are not always verbal. Be careful not to sigh, groan, roll your eyes, shift your weight or change your posture in such a way as to indicate a non-verbal interruption.

- **Wait your turn.** Take turns when communicating in a group discussion. Do not monopolize the speaker's role. It is not always necessary to take a turn speaking about every topic. Show consideration for others in the group by letting everyone share the limelight. If someone who is especially shy or rarely speaks up shows interest in a topic, consider letting them have your speaking turn too.

- **Pay attention.** You are not listening if you are responding in your head while the person is speaking. Pay attention the next time someone is speaking to you. If you notice you have started speaking to yourself in your head, analyzing what they've said or formulating your next comment, you're really not listening. Give yourself time to hear their complete thought and then formulate your response. This is a good way to avoid speaking in haste and saying the wrong thing.

F. Don't take the bait

Sure it's a nice idea to be polite to people, even when they're wrong, or screaming at you, or obviously picking a fight. In reality, it's not always easy to be "the bigger person" and walk away from someone who has deliberately put you in an embarrassing or difficult situation. One way to deal with these situations properly, is to be prepared. First and foremost, it's important that you see them coming. For example, you know that someone may be trying to get a rise out of you when and if they start a conversation with statements like:

- With all due respect…

- This might be out of line…

- May I ask a personal question?

- I hope you don't mind but…

- If I can offer you some advice…

- If you want my opinion…

Fortunately, with a little practise you can watch for these troublesome lines and resist taking the bait. Instead, turn the tables on the "instigator." The most effective thing to do in this situation is to answer an uncomfortable question with a question. Here are some examples:

Let's say you're at lunch with Nosy Nellie and a couple of co-workers. Suddenly, out of the blue, Nellie boldly asks whether or not you've decided to have the plastic surgery you mentioned last week. Instead of turning red and choking on your grilled cheese, you should look directly at Nellie and say in a surprised and slightly offended tone, "What on earth would make you ask me a personal question like that?" Chances are, it will be Nellie who's caught off guard, trying to chew faster so she can either apologize or come up with some sort of reasonable explanation for her rudeness. This is where you watch her squirm for a few minutes and then act "the bigger person" and let her off the hook by saying, "Oh never mind, it's not important anyway." Hopefully, she'll get the message.

What about when someone asks you how much money you make or how much something costs? The best thing to do is to make a joke, obviously embellish, or change the subject. You might try saying, "It's funny you should ask that, I just booked a private jet to Fiji, a little reward for a very profitable quarter."

If you are truly caught off guard—if, for instance someone asks you a difficult question in front of a group while you're doing a presentation, try saying, "Would you mind if we come back to that later?" This allows you to maintain control for the moment and gives you time to think about an answer, or hopefully, everyone will forget the question was even asked.

Finally, to almost any awkward question, you can try responding with "That's a strange question, could you be more specific?" or "I'm not sure I understand the question, would you rephrase it?" This may put the person off, or, at least, you'll buy a little recovery time. In the worst case scenario, it is perfectly acceptable to simply smile and say, "You know, I'm just not comfortable answering that question." This usually results in the questioner saying, "Oh, sorry I asked."

G. Putting a value on civility

Is there really a tangible cost of rudeness to business? Absolutely! Obviously, poor customer service means losing clients and losing money. But, there is another hidden cost that is equally important. Production in the workplace often boils down to teamwork and a lack of civility results in poor communication and the meltdown of relationships. Rudeness also encourages inter-office conflict that in turn results in heightened stress. So, the hidden cost of rudeness to business is a slowdown in efficiency and production.

Alternatively, the benefits of courtesy in the workplace are far reaching, both for the business and for the business professional. Knowing what behavior is acceptable in business and social situations allows us to be confident so we can get down to the business at hand. Good manners are skills that others expect, respect and remember. Finally, courtesy helps to eliminate unfortunate judgment calls that others often make in the work place. Proper business conduct results in increased productivity for the business and career advancement for the individual. In other words, courtesy is a "check" you can take to the bank!

H. Chapter summary

A polished professional understands that a working knowledge of what constitutes "appropriate conduct" in every social and business situation is mandatory in today's competitive business world. Such knowledge allows you to exhibit confidence, maintain your self-respect and build a productive reputation. Good manners and an ability to communicate an attitude of respect and consideration for others are just good business—plain and simple!

Even when you're on the front lines, you're in training for the top. So remember that good business and good manners are compatible—unintentional rudeness is still rudeness! Poise and confidence are essential in every business related situation. Knowing how to remain in control and communicate effectively regardless of the environment or the company is essential. Manners are your attitude set into action! Be aware of your customer service attitude because it's a good indication of how you'll fare in dealing with co-workers and higher ups as you climb the corporate ladder.

Answers to self-assessment:

1. **False.** Always make eye contact with the speaker first. Then make eye contact and acknowledge anyone else who is present.

2. **False.** You should never leave a service situation unless you can refer the client to someone else who can help them.

3. **False.** You should show empathy to the client. They probably don't really care who is at fault for the problem; they just want someone to take responsibility for fixing it.

4. **False.** Customer service includes showing consideration for what impression you make on the client and for considering their comfort. Always dress in "business appropriate" attire.

5. **False.** Just because someone can maintain their composure

does not mean they do not care about an issue. Always take every customer complaint seriously.

6. **False.** Most often angry customers want to vent. Let them speak or yell and don't interrupt them.

7. **True.** If someone is particularly upset, it is always best to take him or her somewhere private, if possible.

8. **True.** Being a good listener is fundamental to determining the actual problem and then resolving it.

9. **True.** You should never make promises you cannot keep just to calm someone down or act like a hero.

10. **False.** To most irate customers, timing is everything. If they are already upset and then they are kept waiting, it will be too little too late.

Answers to office scenarios:

1. You can't be quick enough for Mr. Impatient. Typically, if you are engaged face-to-face or on the telephone with a client and another approaches, immediately make eye contact, smile and acknowledge the approaching client. Then finish your call as quickly as possible and help the walk-in client. In this case, Linda should either ask if the first client minds holding for a moment, and then take a moment to greet the client who has just arrived or, if she feels really pressured by Mr. Impatient, she might try asking to call the telephone client back and helping Mr. Impatient first.

2. Common sense dictates that whether or not anything is said depends entirely on how important the client is to the business. But, if at all possible, someone should say something to Mr. Somebody. His lateness, canceling and rudeness are very poor behavior. If the manager/boss approves, the administrative person who most often deals with him may speak to him politely in private. Maybe he has just developed bad habits, or is unaware of his behavior.

3. Someone had better get a hold of Matthew Mascot. He probably thinks he's helping but he can do a tremendous amount of damage to the company's reputation. Initially, a

co-worker who feels brave enough should speak to Matthew in confidence without criticizing or blaming. Maybe he is totally unaware of how incorrect or inappropriate his behavior is. Maybe he just wants some recognition as a great client and he'll stop the bandwagon behavior if he feels adequately appreciated.

4. It's best to smile and maintain a calm demeanor. Try not to look panicky or alarmed. Simply remove the files and suggest to Ten Fingers Tina that she should not be in the conference room, reiterating that the information is confidential. Maybe, ask her if she had a specific interest in the information. Then look directly at the articles hidden in her coat pocket and give her an opportunity to explain or simply ask her to leave them on the table and follow you out. Then, report/document the incident immediately to your supervisor.

5. Ricky is probably not going to take a hint easily and will most certainly take any response as positive reinforcement. Simply mention the issue to the co-worker or boss and proceed as directed. They may be comfortable handling the situation. If not, you may have to be cruel and suggest to Ricky that the object of his affection is otherwise unavailable or be firm in telling him that you will no longer be able to deal with the "personal issue."

Chapter Two

MOVING ON UP!
Thinking like the boss

Well, now that you've mastered customer service and you understand that your service attitude applies to internal customers too, you're probably thinking you'd like to be the boss. Be careful what you wish for. If you think you work hard now, that your responsibilities are heavy or that you already have difficulty with your co-workers, think carefully about what you really want. And, if you're wondering why you've been passed over for that promotion twice, maybe think about why. Do you know how to handle yourself properly in every business situation? Are you most often positive and energized at work? Do you value your superior and peer relationships? What about problem solving? Are you typically part of the problem or part of the solution? Hmmm? Let's see, if you're really honest about it, do you have what it takes to be the leader of the pack? And, if you haven't earned it yet, are you prepared to make the effort? What does it take anyway? Take the self-assessment and see where you are.

Quiz: Self-assessment

	True or False
Answer true or false to each of the following:	

1. When a project is complete you should take as much credit as possible; people need to know how much you contributed.

2. To ensure a deeper bond with employees, you should share your personal problems with them. They will feel included in your life, which is important to team-building.

3. Whenever possible, you should refuse to listen to gossip and discourage others from passing it along.

4. In dress and decorum, you should emulate the style of a higher-up that you admire.

5. If you are the boss, it is important to keep employees on their toes by interrupting discussions, challenging ideas and questioning decisions. You must always have the upper hand.

6. Joining in an ongoing "complaining session" is necessary occasionally so subordinates will know you can relate to their troubles.

7. When you are sending employees to represent the company, it is their responsibility to look and act like professionals. There is no need to "coach" them; they're adults and can figure it out for themselves.

8. As the boss, you have earned the right to come in late, leave early and take long lunches. Working hard years ago should allow you to have privileges later in your career and you should not have to justify your behavior.

▶

	True or False
9. Adapting your speech style to the people you work with shows you respect and appreciate communication differences.	
10. When you have a problem with an employee, email them. That way you both can handle criticism indirectly.	

(See answers at the end of this chapter.)

A. Getting "it"

How is it that some people just seem to have "it?" From the moment they walk in the room, people are clamoring to talk to them or tripping over themselves to be seen with them. It's painfully obvious that they're a somebody! And how come "the somebody" seems to know everyone? Most often the boss has "it," the guy who just got promoted has "it," and the young up and comer has "it." What is "it" exactly and how can you get "it?"

"It" is mostly just a display of confidence. You may be surprised to discover that everyone, even someone who has "it," gets scared or nervous, just like you. But the difference between the overlords and the underlings is often just a matter of looking cool and acting confident in every situation, even if you don't always feel that way.

B. Never let them see you sweat

One of the reasons certain people advance quickly in business is their uncanny ability to seem in control all of the time. It doesn't take a genius to figure out that the person sulking in the corner, pounding their fists on the table, screaming at team members or obviously stressing out does not garner much confidence or respect from others, particularly if they are the person responsible for leadership and decision-making. Of course, we're all human and even the brightest, most well-organized professionals are going to find themselves in unexpected, difficult or seemingly impossible situations. But, how you handle yourself in such situations is what separates the leaders from the followers. Here are some tips on maintaining control of difficult situations and your reputation:

■ **Get the facts.** Don't panic. Make sure you have all the information before you jump to conclusions. Most often, once you have the facts, things are not as difficult as they might have seemed. Be very careful not to take the opinion of others as fact until you can verify the details. An opinion is only an opinion. Show respect for the speaker but remember opinions are not fact.

■ **Take a time-out.** If you cannot control your emotions, excuse yourself from the situation long enough to regain your composure and then return to the situation.

■ **Face the worst.** Ask yourself, "How bad could it be, really?" Consider the worst thing that could possibly happen. Then, consider how and if you could deal with it and make a decision accordingly. If you are really not capable of handling the situation, get help!

■ **Fast forward, rewind and play it again, Sam.** Don't be too quick to speak. Listen first, take some time to formulate a reasonable action and then choose your words carefully. Use "I" phrases to express an opinion and take responsibility for your thoughts rather than using "we" and speaking for the rest of the group who may not be forthcoming with their own opinions.

■ **Look in the looking glass.** Be aware of your posture, facial expressions and body language. Control your emotions and remember that you can send a message of anger or annoyance without saying anything. Be careful not to wring your hands, adopt a rigid posture, clench your jaw or tap your fingers or foot. All of these cues can indicate displeasure and close the channels of communication, leaving no hope for an amiable conclusion to the problem.

- **Lighten up.** Maintain a sense of humor. Chances are everyone involved in the situation is tense and uptight about it, particularly those who were ultimately responsible for the problem arising in the first place. As a team, the goal is to find a solution, not to point fingers and rehash the how's and why's. Take a "we'll get through this approach" and try to see the humor in the situation. Everyone will feel calmer and be more likely to take a productive approach to solving the problem.

C. Will the real Mr. President please stand: Secrets of professionals

It does not matter whether your chosen field is botany or bifocals, professionals in business need to understand what behaviors are expected and accepted in every possible business situation. It does not matter how many degrees you have or how many years you've been on the job, sooner or later a lack of social intelligence will cost you. If you want to achieve success in business, it is absolutely mandatory that you learn how to communicate confidence and competence. Your behaviors are constantly under examination and you'll need to be conscious of how your actions are affecting your reputation at all times. It may seem obvious, but try to avoid behaviors that will damage your reputation. Here, for example, are some rarely promoted and not too professional characters:

> **JITTERY JEFF:** They're not jumping when Jeff enters a room, they're just jumpy. That's because Jeff is always wandering around fretting and sweating. Bad enough as a co-worker, as a boss, he's got an entire office full of neurotics working under him. Jeff doesn't inspire confidence in his employees because he doesn't have any himself. Remember Jeff, lead by example!

> **MOODY MEL:** Just when you thought today would be a great day, in comes Moody Mel. Yesterday she left laughing but today she arrives moaning. One minute she's singing your praises, the next, she's insinuating that you can't do anything right. It's never easy having Mel for a co-worker never mind a boss, her mood changes every hour…and of course, so does

Did I say good job? I meant good dog!

yours! Stay on your toes and call ahead to see if it's safe to approach. Whatever you do, don't make the mistake of asking how she is—you'll be sorry.

Confidence is not just about appearances. You can gain confidence by developing professional habits that prepare you for any business situation. Stop and think for a moment about someone you know who has had success in business. What is it about them that you admire? There are most certainly "characteristics of professionals," traits that polished business persons carry and habitually practise. Most often, the behaviors are so ingrained that the person does not even realize that they've developed these positive habits. But others do notice and aim to emulate. Here are some qualities or behaviors of a business professional:

- **Straight like a ruler:** Professionals who respect themselves and others make every effort to be direct and to the point whenever possible. Think before you speak and practise your listening skills. As a leader, there will most certainly be times when being right will have to take precedence over being popular.

- **A little change will do you good:** Leaders recognize that adapting to change is necessary and most often leads to a positive outcome. But they also know that resilience does not mean showing weakness or being indecisive. Professionals adjust quickly and effectively and make efforts to see how change impacts the big picture.

- **Risky business:** No one gets anywhere in life without taking a risk or two. Risk in business means considering whether you can afford not to take a particular chance and weighing the consequences before you make decisions.

- **Monkey see, monkey don't do:** Chances are you're not the first person to have to deal with the decision at hand. That is why smart professionals watch and learn. You can indeed learn from the mistakes of others rather than making the mistake yourself.

- **Open for business:** Leaders are open-minded. They are good listeners and hesitate to dismiss any logically presented idea—you never know where something might lead. Progressive professionals who want to move ahead keep up with the times. They are open to new ideas and are often the first in line to learn new tasks and try new things. Another important point is that open-minded people are not immediately threatened by people who offer new ideas.

- **A stitch in time:** If you want to be in charge, you have to act like you're in charge and in control. This is easier to do when you're prepared. Take the time to do your research and put necessary information into a professional, productive format. If you are not prepared, don't make excuses and don't expect others to cover for you.

- **Know your product; know your client:** No-one is going to buy your product if you cannot speak intelligently about it or present it effectively. Make a point of finding out what exactly your client needs and adapt your product accordingly.

- **The batteries are still running:** Feeling and acting energized is a sure fire way to show others you feel positively about who you are and what you're trying to do. Take care of yourself physically and the rest is sure to follow. You cannot expect others to be energized or excited about being around you if you are not positive and exciting to be around.

- **One step ahead of the game:** Leaders solve many problems by anticipating them before they happen. Have a plan and think it through. Don't leave things to chance and keep your cool if things happen to get out of control.

- **I think I can! I think I can!** Be the little engine that could. If you want to be the leader, you have to believe you can be. Act confident and you'll look and feel and be confident! You probably don't have to go so far as to hum "walking on sunshine…." all day long but if you can't act like a professional and lead by example, you better think twice about your aspirations on becoming the boss.

- **Just say thank you:** Nothing says professional and confident like taking a compliment gracefully. If you're going to be the boss, be positive and learn to take a compliment as well as to give them freely. It's going to take a lot of hard work to be the leader of the pack and you deserve to be recognized for it. Do not point out your weaknesses or the weaknesses of others and never be afraid to say something positive. Leaders who have the confidence to take credit for their accomplishments while acknowledging the efforts of others set a good example and encourage productivity.

D. Pretty is as pretty does: Check your attitude

When you look like you are confident and in control, and when you've learned professional habits that make you feel more confident, it's time to start inspiring confidence in others. The number one way to encourage your co-workers, employees and employers to feel confident about your abilities is by being consistent in your behaviors. If others know that you are always calm, approachable, and can be trusted to react in a professional manner in any situation, you will inspire confidence and become a leader. The best way to develop this kind of consistency is to maintain a positive attitude. Here are some tips:

- **Get it together.** Be neutral or be positive. If you try hard enough, there is always something positive you can say. If not, smile and listen respectfully to the opinions of others. You can always say, "That's interesting," or "I'll have to give that some thought," and save your opinion for a more appropriate time. Besides, there are times when silence is power.

- **That was my evil twin talking.** Ask a close friend or family member to tell you if you have any "tells." These are physical characteristics or behaviors that betray your emotions and you may not even be aware of them. Maybe you clench your jaw when you're angry, maybe your ears turn red when you're tired, or maybe you inadvertently shake your knee when you're nervous. Don't forget how much communication is non-verbal. It's important to control it if you can and keep your emotions in check.

- **Oh this old thing.** Purposely identify the attributes of others and point them out. It's strange that people are often conservative with their praise, considering how much they enjoy being praised themselves. Be spontaneous. If you really feel grateful for something someone has done, say so! If you are genuinely impressed by someone's service or presentation or attitude, go out of your way to tell them or send a note. You'll both feel great.

- **And if I wave my magic wand.** Remember you cannot control other people's behavior, you can only control your reaction to their behavior. There are times when you will have to take the high road. Sometimes there is just no point in arguing or pointing out an error or giving someone the satisfaction of reacting to his or her behavior. Pick your battles carefully and try not to let the little things bother you.

- **You know what they say about a-s-s-u-m-e.** Do not underestimate people or take them for granted. Make sure you have all the facts and if you don't know something, ask!

- **The sky is falling, the sky is falling!** Do not always assume the worst. One of the reasons we often find ourselves on the defensive is because we have a tendency to jump to conclusions. Think about what goes through your head when the boss's number shows up on your home call display. The same applies to being approached by a client who may not seem in a good mood. We assume the worst and we're automatically on the attack.

- **I'm here now so let the party begin.** There is no such thing as fashionably late. If you will be late, call! There is nothing more disrespectful than taking someone else's time for granted. Being late and then making excuses or even worse, making no apology, does not leave a positive impression.

- **Just breathe.** Pause purposefully. Take a moment to compose yourself and gather your thoughts when you walk into a new situation or environment. This allows you to take a deep breath, think productive thoughts and present yourself in a positive light.

- **Oops, did I say that out loud?** Be mindful of where you are and who may be listening or watching. Be very careful about letting that negative energy out. Temper, temper! A burst of tension expressed by slamming the door or kicking the vending machine can leave you with some explaining to do if witnessed by the wrong person. Similarly, don't speak negatively in the elevator or corporate washroom, the parking lot, the corner store by the office or even the staff lunchroom.

E. Time is money! Time management tips

Etiquette is all about showing respect and consideration for others. As a leader, it's important to remember this not only applies to your clients but your employees as well. One important and simple way to show respect in business is to show respect for time. Respect the time of others and your own. Here are the top five rules for time management:

1. First and foremost, don't bite off more than you can chew. Don't book more than you can handle and always leave room for the unexpected. Being selective about what you can fit into your schedule means taking a moment to assess what needs to be done and learning to priorize.

2. Organize your schedule, confirm your appointments and verify details related to location, attendance and agenda. Arrive a few minutes early whenever you can. This allows you to check your notes and check out the environment where you'll be working. You can then anticipate and/or resolve any potential problem that might arise. You'll save a lot of time in the end.

3. Take notes. Highlighting the key purpose and points of a meeting helps you focus on your priorities so that you don't waste time rehashing irrelevant details. Plus, taking notes shows others that you're interested, listening and have some intention of following through.

4. Think before you speak. Give yourself a few minutes to absorb the materials, think carefully about your response and then say it out loud. Think how much time is wasted when hasty responses result in aimless banter and repeated efforts at clarification.

5. Finally, don't try to be superhuman. When in a group scenario, we often feel the need to take on additional responsibilities just to show we're capable or that we're a team player. Resist the urge to show off and remember that it's far better to do a few things really well than it is to do many things poorly.

F. Small talk, big meaning

Small talk can be just as important as "official" business conversation and can teach you a lot about your clients, co-workers, or employees. Even in the most casual exchanges, be sure to listen and ask questions so that you are sure you understand the speaker. Don't be shy about asking for reiteration if you've missed something. By the same token, make sure you observe the speaker carefully and pay attention to non-verbal cues that can help you "read between the lines." Don't forget you can learn a lot about a person through trivial conversation and by watching non-verbal communication cues carefully during seemingly unimportant exchanges.

The tone of your small talk is also important; it tells clients, co-workers and employees something about you. Don't be afraid to show your human side now and then. Have a repertoire of great, non-work-related stories about your experiences and your life. Great stories are true, based on personal experience, descriptive yet not pretentious, typically include some humor and shouldn't be too long. Telling something about yourself that others can relate to reminds them that although you may be more accomplished than they, you are still human. Don't get too personal of course; you want them to respect you in the morning.

As a professional at any level, it is vital to recognize that every interaction, every single minute spent in communication with clients and co-workers solicits a reaction. Try to consistently keep in mind that the minutes count and it's often the details that have the greatest influence. Accordingly, make every conversation count. A sincere greeting carries tremendous impact and can be reinforced by a deliberate "thank you for your efforts" or "I appreciate your time" on the way out. Simple common courtesies take little time or effort and can make all the difference.

G. Adam and Eve, they both took a ribbing: A note on gender communications

Monitoring your own communication habits as you take on more responsibility and climb the corporate ladder can be a complicated issue. Having to decipher the styles of others and consider rank can also increase stress levels. Add to that the obvious differences between men and women's communication styles and communication can be extremely difficult, even impossible at times.

It's no secret that men and women communicate differently. Success in modern workplace environments means working and communicating with co-workers and clients including the opposite sex at all levels of the corporate ladder. Understanding how people communicate can increase productivity and build strong mixed gender teams. Many interpersonal conflicts between peers, higher ups and clients can be avoided if we take time to understand communication differences. On the next page is a list of "communication behaviors" that the Etiquette Ladies have noticed are typical for a particular gender. Now, don't panic. We don't always display these gender specific behaviors, but 4000 self-help books on gender can't be wrong. See if you can guess which sex most often exhibits each behavior.

Being aware of common "gender specific" behaviors gives us an opportunity to anticipate actions and to react accordingly. Just as you understand that a person who is consistently late will always be late and you don't take the behavior personally, understanding behaviors that both men and women commonly exhibit helps eliminate unfair judgments. And in anticipating behaviors, a polished professional can adapt their own behavior accordingly.

QUIZ: GENDER COMMUNICATIONS

	Women or Men
Answer "Women" or "Men" for the following:	
1. ...often give compliments related to appearance.	
2. ...have a tendency to apologize for things beyond their control.	
3. ...are often comfortable taking credit for achievements.	
4. ...tend to show emotion when speaking and/or through non-verbal communication.	
5. ...are not always comfortable discussing personal issues like family or health.	
6. ...need to be acknowledged immediately through handshakes or eye contact before initiating conversation.	
7. ...will sometimes be comfortable taking your word for it.	
8. ...generally give longer, more detailed explanations.	
9. ...have difficulty taking a compliment.	
10. ...more often use slang or swearwords to make a point.	
11. ...are more likely to use humor to break tension.	
12. ...typically speak figuratively and expect you to read between the lines.	
13. ...prefer to discuss business and then socialize.	
14. ...tend to be more careful about stepping on someone else's toes.	
15. ...will likely come straight to the point regardless of the sensitivity of the issue.	
16. ...more often require "tangible" follow-up documentation.	

(See answers at the end of this chapter.)

H. Chapter summary

When it comes to climbing the corporate ladder, everyone needs some of "it." In business circles, "it" refers to polish or professionalism, which is exhibited by some specific behaviors, most notably exhibiting confidence. Confidence can be gained through etiquette skills, including monitoring your attitude, adapting your communication style, controlling your emotions, and showing respect for time. It seems like a lot to accomplish, but it's not that complicated if you get in the habit of thinking before you act. Specifically, think about how you can show care, respect and consideration for others before you think about yourself. Courtesy is "it" and you'll reap the rewards by practising "it."

Answers to self-assessment:

1. **False.** If there is a team involved, make sure that everyone gets equal credit for their effort.

2. **False.** Regardless of your position, keep your personal life as private as possible.

3. **True.** Gossip is very uncivilized behavior in any situation and it ruins careers.

4. **True.** It is smart to emulate the people you aspire to be like.

5. **False.** Bosses who manage effectively understand that encouraging people is far more productive than discouraging them.

6. **False.** Very rarely are significant problems actually addressed in complaining sessions.

7. **False.** If the individual will represent the company, they are representing you too, and you should take care to give them the guidance they need.

8. **False.** As the boss, you may have earned the right to act without justifying your behavior, however, you should always lead by example. The "do as I say, not as I do" approach does not get you much credibility.

9. **True.** It is respectful to speak in a manner that is clearly understood by the person to whom you are speaking.

10. **False.** Never send emotional messages or details regarding confidential issues by email. It is far more professional and respectful to speak to the individual in person.

Answers to gender quiz:

1. Women

2. Women

3. Men

4. Women

5. Men

6. Women

7. Men

8. Women

9. Women

10. Men

11. Men

12. Women

13. Men

14. Women

15. Men

16. Women

Chapter Three

PACK YOUR BAGS, NOT YOUR BAGGAGE: Business travel

D oesn't everyone's dream job include luxurious all expense paid trips to exotic locations, gourmet four-course meals on the company credit card, a little spare time by the pool—on the clock of course—and delightful clients that shower you with thoughtful gifts? Yeah right! That's why they call it a dream job. Keep dreaming, because for most of us travel for work really means a two-hour commute, exotic locations are rural towns with only one restaurant where you're lucky to get a good grilled cheese sandwich, there's never any free time, and the expense allotment barely covers your gas. Corporate gifts, uuuggh! How many baseball caps and monogrammed golf tees can one gal use?

Nevertheless, if you're moving up that corporate ladder, you'll probably be doing a lot of business travel. Whether it's the town twenty minutes away or a conference in Hawaii, every minute that you are away for business you are representing the company and you have to be on your best behavior. In fact, the more you travel and are away from the office, the more you prove your ability to handle responsibility and decision-making on your own—qualities that make you promotion worthy. Are you ready for a ticket to paradise and/or a move up that ladder? Take the self-assessment and find out.

Quiz: Self-assessment

	True or False
Answer true or false to each of the following:	
1. As a follow-up gesture, you should send thank-you notes to individuals or organizations that make your traveling experience or business trip more comfortable.	
2. When you're traveling for business, you're not really on the clock so it's okay to let your hair down, put on a comfy sweatshirt and jeans, and plan to relax until you arrive at the conference.	
3. If possible, try to avoid checking your baggage. That's what overhead bins are for and it's your personal convenience that matters most.	
4. You should always consume as much wine as possible when your are being entertained for business. Everyone wants you to enjoy yourself and you should be sure to get your money's worth.	
5. It's much easier to conduct business with associates from different cities/countries if you've researched the places/people/ company you're visiting.	
6. When you are in a new city or country, people will forgive tardiness as they can appreciate that you don't know your way around.	
7. If you have to purchase toiletries or magazines for personal use at the hotel gift shop, it's okay to charge it on the company card because you're on company time.	
8. If you are traveling with co-workers, you can feel free to pass on details about your traveling companion's sleeping habits, medication, or personal details when you return home.	▶

	True or	False
9. If you are staying at the home of a business associate, you should try to gather details about their likes and dislikes so that you can send an appropriate thank-you gift.		
10. Try to hug as many people as you can when you leave a conference, airport or hotel, so that others will know you are approachable and that you enjoyed yourself.		

(See answers at the end of this chapter.)

A. Pick me! How to become one of the chosen

When you travel for business, you are representing the company. That's why the person chosen isn't necessarily the first person who's available or the one who most wants to go. So who does get chosen to represent the company at the annual conference in Florida? And what is it that determines whether or not you'll be seated next to the company president when you attend that awards dinner in Montreal? It should be obvious but unfortunately it's not. If you're wondering why you're spending spring break in the mail room while your associates are off to a trade show in Bermuda, you might want to ask yourself the following questions. Chances are your higher ups have already asked these questions, and chances are they didn't get the answers they wanted.

Can you say "yes" to the following?

1. Do you look and act like a professional at all times?

2. Do you speak highly of the company and of higher ups?

3. Can you be trusted to show up on time for work and meetings during the normal course of the day?

4. Do you go out of your way to be friendly with clients?

5. Are you even-tempered and cooperative with co-workers?

6. Can you be trusted to make reasonable and responsible decisions on the fly?

7. Are you responsible with your expense account?

8. How are your communication skills? Could you get a message across to someone if there were a language barrier?

9. What about presentation skills? Could you be called upon in an impromptu situation to speak about the company and products?

10. Do you actually know enough about your employer, the client in question, the issues at hand or the problem in question to adequately represent the company on your own away from the safety of your office?

Can you say "no" to the following?

1. Are you afraid to introduce yourself or initiate conversations in mingling situations?

2. Do you behave differently when you think no-one's watching?

3. Do you take advantage of company time, you know, bend the rules a little, take long lunches?

4. Have you been known to act inappropriately in social situations? Do you eat too much, drink too much or flirt too much?

When you're in business, it's important to remember that everyone is watching, even if you can't see them. If you're not careful about your behavior at the office, how can they trust you when you're away?

B. The plane truth: 14 Travel tips

Okay, so let's say you're one of the lucky ones. Many first time company fliers forget that when you're traveling for business, you should always be "on." In fact, when you're moving up that ladder and finding more of your business and personal life blending together, you need to be "on" nearly all the time. A business trip is a great way for you and your company to find out if you have what it takes to be the boss.

If you are, in fact, chosen to represent the company, you've just accepted a huge responsibility. Want to ensure that your first business trip is not your last? Here are 14 time-honored tips for first time company fliers:

1. **Be grateful!** You've waited a long time for this opportunity, so plan to take advantage of it.

2. **Be conscious of your appearance and demeanor.** When you're catching a plane to go somewhere for business, dress as though you were going to work and act professionally.

3. **Be courteous and polite to everyone you meet.** This includes the taxi driver, the baggage handler, the ticket taker, the flight attendant and other travelers you may meet. You never know whose assistance you'll end up needing or who you'll end up spending time with. Treat everyone like you'd treat your clients.

4. **Be prepared.** Check flight times in advance. Leave early so you don't have to rush. Double check that you have all your personal belongings and any necessary professional documents. Make sure your carry-on luggage bag is the acceptable size, tag your bags and wait politely in the check-in line with everyone else.

5. **Take care of yourself.** If you need a cup of coffee to function, get one. If you have a cold, get some lozenges so you won't cough annoyingly during the entire flight.

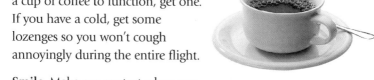

6. **Smile.** Make eye contact when you meet people, especially your seatmates.

7. **Follow the rules.** Wear your seatbelt and don't give the service people a hard time just because you're in a bad mood.

8. **Don't be a chatterbox.** Carry on polite conversation with your neighbor but don't talk incessantly if it's obvious someone is trying to work, read or sleep.

9. **Be brief in the bathroom.** Keep in mind that there are others who may require the use of the facilities. And don't forget to clean up after yourself, flush, and wash your hands.

10. **Mind your personal space.** Try not to take up more than your share of the space provided. Keep your elbows and feet within your allotted seat space and don't sleep if you know you snore loudly, talk in your sleep, drool or have a tendency to borrow someone's shoulder for a pillow.

11. **Think before you drink.** If you will be picked up by an associate or client, think twice about drinking alcohol on the plane. Some people's systems react poorly to liquor at high altitudes and if first impressions are at stake…

12. **Be positive and tactful.** Don't speak loudly or rudely about other passengers, the incidence of airplanes crashing, the weather, your work or other inappropriate topics. You never know who is listening.

13. **Keep it private.** Be careful about working on the laptop or reading confidential company papers in public places, including the airplane. You never know who's looking over your shoulder.

14. **Be patient.** When the plane comes to rest, let those ahead of you deplane first and don't push or shove. It wouldn't hurt to offer assistance to anyone who seems to be struggling with their bags either.

It seems like a lot to remember but when you're traveling for business, image is everything. Imagine getting bumped to first class and having to sit next to the CEO of Company XYZ who you've been trying desperately to have return your phone calls.

How confident will you feel in your backwards baseball cap and sweatpants? Remember though, your image is more than how you're dressed. How you conduct yourself—decorum—is relevant too. Even if you are dressed in khakis and sandals, you can present yourself positively through your behavior and speech style. Treating everyone with consideration and respect will go a long way to sprucing up your image. It never hurts to dress up a little though, just in case.

C. Ready, set… Being prepared

Remember, the key to real confidence is actually knowing what you're doing. Whether you're traveling to New Brunswick, New York, or New Delhi, as a business professional, you need to be prepared. It is essential and respectful to research your destination, make lists and take notes. Whenever possible, try to become familiar with the area and the people you will be surrounded by. You're kidding yourself if you think that just because you're staying at the hotel for the trade show, what's going on around you is not relevant. There are many things you can do to ensure that you're ready to meet any challenge which may arise when you reach your destination. Here are a few suggestions to help you plan for the success of your next business trip:

- **Know who's who.** Try to find out in advance of your arrival who is on the guest list for functions, meetings, dinners, etc. that you will be attending. You may even consider getting a complete agenda prior to the trip and researching other companies who may be attending.

- **Call ahead.** Confirm bookings, reservations and appointments. You don't want to arrive at the Great Hotel only to discover that your reservation was actually for the Grande Hotel, which happens to be a 45-minute drive away. It's a good idea to check out the locations of appointments and final destinations in advance of the scheduled meetings just to be sure.

- **Anticipation won't keep you waiting.** Car breaks down, flight's delayed, train derails. It's very important to anticipate every possible thing that could go wrong and have a Plan B prepared. Always take pertinent phone numbers and contact information, a little extra cash and a change of clothes with you in your carry-on luggage, just in case.

- **Give it away.** Prepare and bring along appropriate gifts. If you've researched your client, you may have discovered something about them—they have children, for example, or particular hobbies—which makes gift giving much easier. Be careful not to be overly generous or too frugal as both can result in uncomfortable situations.

- **Make a note.** Keep an empty space in your daybook to jot down details, notes and reminders, which you will need to follow up with when you return home. Thank-you cards, packages, and unanswered questions should all be addressed within seven days of your return.

- **Be cash conscious.** Evaluate your budget in advance of your trip. Review the budget carefully with the "keeper of the cash or credit" to ensure that you know your limitations prior to your trip. Find out exactly what you're allowed to spend, what are acceptable expenses, and for what you will be personally responsible. Chances are that new sun hat you purchased at the hotel gift boutique will not be an allowable corporate expense.

Who was it who first said, "Failing to plan is planning to fail"? If you don't do your research you just may end up like one of these unfortunate business travelers:

TRINA THE TOURIST: Click, click, click. Trina's more interested in the doorman's sightseeing directions than the directions to the trade show. She's camera-happy and asking a million questions, not about the competition but about where to go shopping! The only reason she visits the convention center at all is to gather free trinkets for everyone back home. If the boss knew she actually wears her corporate name tag on her Hawaiian shirt…. Yikes, you'd never know she was traveling for business.

PACK-A-LOT PAT:
Good gravy! You'd guess Pat's moving to Mexico. She's packed enough to clothe 10 people for at least two months, no laundry service required. She's only going for five days. Can a person wear 12 different hats in five days? It takes two helpers just to get her luggage to the

Oww, ohhh my back!

elevator. I guess we'll know who to find if we need a blender, toaster or extra coffee maker. Better plan on her being late for early meetings—wardrobe decisions take time.

D. All work and no play…

When it comes to traveling for business, most bosses would agree that although they want you to accomplish the business at hand, they also want you to enjoy yourself. This being said, let's be reasonable. A couple of drinks with a client is one thing, an all night bender is quite another. Maybe it's reasonable to skip out one afternoon to play golf, but it's entirely unreasonable to show up an hour late for the gala dinner in your golf shoes. Always remember, it's business! Most everyone gets more work done if they're relatively comfortable and relaxed, but there's a fine line. Be careful not to cross it. Know your boundaries and learn how to bow out graciously. Keep in mind that sometimes clients extend invitations for the sake of being courteous and you are not really expected to accept.

E. Make manners your destination: International protocol

Once you've moved up either in the eyes of your boss or in the company, you might just be lucky enough to travel the globe. But before you get too wound up, remember that international travel brings up a whole host of possible etiquette blunders. These might not be so bad if you're a tourist, but when you travel for business, the company's reputation—and yours—is on the line. When you venture out of the office for an international trip, be sure to find out about each of the following in the country you will be visiting:

- Appropriate business attire

- Gender relations

- Proper use and presentation of business cards

- Gift-giving and receiving

- Attitude towards business and alcohol

- Toasting

- Dining and culture-specific foods

- Acceptable body language and gestures

- Personal habits

- Greetings and making an exit

- Time frames for building relationships

- Humor and joke-telling

- Forms of address

- Business hours and days of business

- Special holidays

- Role of spouse and partner

- Negotiating behaviors

Doing your research ahead of time is important whenever you travel but moreso on business. However, as we stated earlier, it's not just business you'll be doing on your business trip. Knowing social customs is important too. The following six handy tips will be useful not only for business travel but pleasure trips as well. Remember, good etiquette habits become part of your life. Here we go:

1. **Bring a map.** Make sure you know where you are relative to where you need to go. Asking someone in Mexico City how far Puerto Vallarta is because you were considering going for lunch is just plain stupidity.

2. **Be informed.** Get on the net or go to the library prior to your trip and learn a little about where you're going. This includes general information about famous residents, sporting teams and events, festivals, religious holidays, local customs, etc.

3. **Get cultured.** It's important to know a little of the history and culture of the area. Just as we as Canadians resent visitors presuming that we all live in igloos, it's ignorant and disrespectful not to learn a little about where you're going. Keep in mind that culture varies within the country as well and be careful not to generalize.

4. **Speak their language.** If traveling out of the country, try to learn a few key phrases in the language of your destination. This will show your interest in the people you will be dealing with and help you communicate. People generally appreciate efforts to speak their language and will overlook the expected mispronunciations. Don't forget, body language is important. A smile is recognized in any language.

5. **Bide your time.** When it comes to appointments, be mindful of what is acceptable in different countries—sometimes it may be construed as incredibly rude to be late where

other's may see it as incredibly rude to be early. Check it out in advance.

6. **Keep it current.** It's extremely important to know something about the currency you'll be using. You wouldn't want to be caught short with only 1000 pesos having just found out that what you thought was a small fortune is only worth a few dollars!

It is the Etiquette Ladies dream to be able to experience every country and culture and eventually write about their first hand discoveries. For now, however, we are happy to share these examples of business deals gone awry due to lack of research and misinterpreted gestures. We secretly followed "Bumbling Bob" from country to country and bring this update on his traveling travesties.

Bumbling Bob is off to Mexico! He's looking forward to dinner at the home of a long-term business associate. Meaning well, he stops to pick up a beautiful bouquet of yellow Gerbera daisies to present to the hostess. Upon his arrival, the faces of his hosts as well as the mood of the party switch instantly from festive to forlorn. Bob has presented the hostess with thoughtful flowers, which happen to be in a color that his Mexican friends associate with death. Poor, poor Bob.

Next stop Thailand. At the end of a long but productive work day, Bumbling Bob pats a colleague on the head to acknowledge a job well done. Oh Bob, if you only knew that in Thailand, the head is considered the most intimate part of the body. Another dinner alone. Aren't you getting tired of your own company, Bob?

Venturing off to Hong Kong, Bumbling Bob has been practising his bowing in the airport bathroom. Confident that he's got his technique down pat, he's off to meet his new clients. You can imagine their surprise when Bob shows off his bowing skills. Bob, Bob, Bob, pay attention. An extended hand should have been your first clue that you're not in Japan where bowing is the custom. Chinese business people shake hands.

Time to cool off Bob, a slow boat to Iceland should do it. What were we thinking? Bumbling Bob rides again. After a superb dinner and impeccable service, Bob knows he's sealed the deal. That is until he makes a grand gesture and plunks down an exorbitant tip. He'll be getting the cold shoulder—tipping is not common or acceptable practice in Iceland.

You just can't win with Bob. Maybe it's time for a little fun. What better place than Italy. Sambuca and sunshine. Lucky Bob's been invited to a social gathering and he's hoping to make some new contacts. Funny, no one seems to want to talk to him. Maybe it's because he persists in asking everyone what he or she does for a living immediately after introducing himself. Italians consider this behavior gauche and extremely insulting.

Well Bob's pretty much worn out his welcome but we're giving him one last chance. Let's see if he can behave himself in Argentina. He's on his best behavior and eager to make a good impression. He arrives at a scheduled business dinner 15 minutes early. Alarmed to find himself alone in the banquet hall, he paces and when the hostess and other guests arrive 30 minutes late, he rushes over to greet them. Not aware that it's the custom to be late, Bob puts his foot in his mouth when he foolishly comments, "I guess I'm the only one with a watch, ha ha."

So what's our point? We live in a world of diversity and varied customs and traditions. If you're fortunate enough to travel for business, make a point of checking out classes and training sessions on the etiquette and protocol of your destination country. This includes everything from non-verbal communication to physical gestures, gender relations, social graces and business dining. If you'll be negotiating or actually planning to close a deal, we highly recommend the extra effort necessary to win the respect both you and your company deserve.

F. How to make a graceful landing

Home again, home again! Don't even think about resting. If you're lucky enough to have a day off after traveling for business, take full advantage. Probably, like the rest of us, your flight will arrive home at midnight on Sunday and you'll be expected to arrive at work bright-eyed and bushy-tailed at 8:30 sharp on Monday morning. If you haven't already done so, it may be wise to stay up an hour or two and review your trip. Chances are the boss and maybe others will be expecting a full report of who you saw and what you learned. If you're smart, you'll be ready. Here are some things to consider when you prepare for that report:

- Review the goals and directives that were outlined prior to the trip. Hopefully you'll have kept a journal and documented any information pertinent to these goals.

- If your company adheres to a specific report format, follow suit and apply your notes accordingly.

- Keep every receipt and document, including boarding passes and marketing materials you may have been given.

- If you took photographs of sites, delegates or events, try to get them developed and copied as soon as possible.

- Have a listing of contacts and client information prepared. You can also use this listing to send out thank-you cards and small gifts if appropriate.

- Set sufficient time aside for the follow-up meeting and be prepared to answer questions. Maybe arrange for your voicemail or administrative people to instruct clients that you will be unavailable until the following day so you can concentrate on tying up loose ends from your trip.

- Be positive in speaking about the trip, the clients and everything else. If there were problems, have solutions or explanations in mind before you bring them up.

- Thank whoever determined that you should take the trip in the first place and let them know how much you appreciated their confidence in you as well as the opportunity.

G. Chapter summary

Two blocks or two time zones, it doesn't matter where you're going; when you're traveling for business, pack your values along with your valuables. Although technology has brought us all closer together, we are still far apart in many ways. Where geographical and linguistic barriers prevail, manners and respect can bridge the distance.

The business trip is the perfect chance for you to present your readiness for promotion. So don't blow it. Be prepared, be aware and be polite. Then you won't have to say, "Pass the Promotion, Please," they'll have already handed it to you on a silver platter.

Answers to self-assessment:

1. **True.** It is very good business to follow up with a handwritten thank-you card.

2. **False.** You should remember that you are always representing the company; dress and act the part at all times.

3. **False.** Whenever possible, think about how to show consideration for others. Cramming bags and parcels into small spaces or invading someone else's personal space is not polite behavior.

4. **False.** You may certainly have a drink, but remember that you are representing the company. Do not take advantage of the hospitality and be careful not to drink too much. Remember first impressions.

5. **True.** It is courteous and respectful to know a little about the people and places you will be dealing with in advance.

6. **False.** There is never a good excuse for being late. Do some research and arrive early.

7. **False.** Items purchased for personal reasons are not the responsibility of the company.

8. **False.** Professionals remember that personal integrity is important and they respect the privacy of others.

9. **True.** Without snooping, it is always thoughtful to be attentive and pay attention to someone's likes so you can send a thoughtful gift.

10. **False.** When you are traveling for business, keep a business attitude. Hugging is too personal; stick to handshakes.

Chapter Four

MOVE OVER MARTHA!
Wine and dining manners

I f you've learned one thing by now it's that in business, you're always on! The higher up you go, the more likely you'll have business time spilling over into social time—and that's not just power lunches and business receptions. You'll be attending banquets, giving toasts and, most likely, you'll be eating in finer, more formal restaurants. If you're serious about the climb, you may as well know now how to handle these situations ahead of time. Sure, the closest you get to fine wine now may be sniffing the screw top and saying "bonne," but, if you play your cards right, you'll be enjoying the nectar of the gods some day. Are you ready? Take the self-assessment and find out.

Quiz: Self-assessment

1. Cell phones, purses, cigarettes etc. should be placed:
   a) to the left of your place setting.
   b) in the center of the table.
   c) under your chair or table.

2. When you are hosting a dining event at a public place, you should:
   a) arrive early and wait for your guests at the table.
   b) leave your name at the desk but arrive after all guests are present.
   c) greet guests at the door and be seated with them.

3. If an invitation states "reception at 6:00":
   a) arrive on time, not late, and never more than 10 minutes early.
   b) arrive by 5:30, you never know if the staff need extra direction.
   c) arrive late. A grand entrance is essential when you want others to feel your importance. Wave and blow kisses to all your fans and admirers.

4. Your fork is accidentally knocked onto the floor. You:
   a) dive to the ground, rescue the utensil, wipe it off with your napkin and continue as though nothing has happened.
   b) start eating with your spoon until a server catches on and brings you another fork.
   c) make eye contact or politely distract the server, request a fork and have them rescue the wayward utensil.

5. Serving bowls and plates should be passed:
   a) clockwise to your left.
   b) counter clockwise to your right.
   c) to whomever shouts out for a particular item.

6. You have been waiting five minutes for a second cup of coffee. You should:
   a) show your domineering or powerful side and berate the service person. Maybe ask loudly, "What does a person have to do to get a bloody cup of coffee around here?"

▶

b) do without. Do you really need the caffeine anyway?

c) approach the host or manager and request a cup of coffee. Try something like, "I realize the server is extremely busy. But I would appreciate a cup of coffee as I have to get back to work shortly."

7. You order your favorite salad and when it arrives, you are terribly distraught to discover that the much-anticipated feta cheese is rancid. You should:

a) chew and swallow, don't make a fuss, pick around and find the lettuce without cheese on it.

b) call the server over and give him an earful. That will teach him to serve this horrid excuse for a salad.

c) as subtly as possible, put your napkin to your mouth and discreetly spit the rancid portion out. Then ask the server to bring you another, fresher salad.

8. When you are ready to depart after dinner, place your napkin on the:

a) chair.

b) right side of the place setting.

c) left side of the place setting.

9. Generally utensils are used from the:

a) inside out.

b) outside in.

c) whatever, it doesn't matter as long as you use them.

10. The proper way to butter a bun is to:

a) cut it in half with a knife, butter both sides and take small bites carefully to avoid getting butter and crumbs on your lips.

b) tear it open with your hands, butter one half completely and eat it, then repeat this for the other half.

c) cut it completely with a knife or make a small indentation with your thumb and finger to separate it, depending on the texture of the bread or bun. Then, tear off bite-sized portions and butter them as you eat them.

(See answers at the end of this chapter.)

A. A fork in the road: Details of dining

So what is the big deal about using the right fork anyway? The etiquette ladies maintain that modern dining etiquette is not about being perfect or "prissy" and we certainly don't want to reinforce old notions that manners are snobby and reserved for "high class" places only. Modern manners, including those for the table, are all about showing care and consideration for others.

Mealtime manners can become increasingly complicated depending on the situation. A formal four- or five-course dinner certainly requires some finesse, especially if there are four or five wines to accompany the food. But there are some simple things to remember about dining etiquette that can apply to every situation. Here are ten handy tips:

1. **Follow the leader.** Do not touch anything on the table—not your napkin, wine, water or buns, not anything—until the host or head of the table has been seated. In lieu of an official host, the most senior person at the table would function as the host. You should wait until this person gives cues as to where others should sit, when the meal starts, who will initiate toasts or speeches and the overall pace of the meal.

2. **Say grace.** One thing to keep in mind is that someone may bless the meal. Even if you don't typically say grace yourself, it is polite to sit in silence if someone else does. If you're the one responsible for saying grace, be aware that others may not be comfortable, so keep it short. No one needs a sermon on an empty stomach.

3. **Know your napkin.** When the host does so, take your napkin and put it in your lap. Fold the napkin in half with the opening towards your stomach—this way you can slip your fingers between the folds to wipe off grease or food bits and your neighbors won't have to see all the "treasure" in your napkin. Use the outside edges of your napkin to dab, not wipe, your mouth and then place the napkin back on your lap. If you must leave during the meal but you will return,

place your napkin on your chair. If you will not be returning, place your napkin to the left of your plate.

4. **Where it is.** Your bread plate is on the left and your glassware is on the right. If someone inadvertently takes your side plate or glass, simply ask the server to bring you another. If you are served soup, either hot or cold, use the larger spoon, which should be on the outside right of your place setting. On some occasions the soupspoon will be served with the soup so don't panic if you don't have one.

5. **Passing.** Always pass to the right, counterclockwise. If you reach for something, maybe buns or butter, be sure to pass the item first and wait until it comes back around before you help yourself. This also applies to salt and pepper which, incidentally, should always be passed together. Handle them from the bottom when you pass them.

6. **'Tis the seasoning.** If you wish to add salt and pepper to your food, do so only after sampling it. It can be incredibly insulting to a chef who has toiled over a meal if you automatically add condiments to the food without having tasted it first.

7. **Bun basics.** Hold your bun or bread over your bread plate and butter bite-sized pieces as you eat them. You should put a pat of butter onto your bread plate using the butter knife or a utensil that hasn't been in your mouth.

8. **Pace yourself.** Take small bites and chew with your mouth closed. Only make comments on the food if they are positive and try to engage in periodic conversation during the meal.

9. **Take a break.** If you pause between bites, be sure to put your utensils all the way on the plate. Don't let them dangle or lean off of the plate and try not to put dirty utensils on the table or the linen.

10. **You're done.** When you are finished eating, don't push your plates to the center of the table or stack them, especially in a

formal dining situation. Instead, lay your utensils across the plate and wait for the server to remove them. Your napkin should stay in your lap until all the food, including dessert, is off of the table.

Just in case you're one of the skeptical that doesn't think anyone really notices poor dining habits, we'd like you to meet some of these all-too memorable dining companions.

HARRY THE HARPOONIST: No need to worry about Harry going hungry, and if you want that last piece of steak, you'd better be quick about eating it. Harry can harpoon up to four feet across any table and you'll never see his fork coming. Before you can say, "Hey, I was going to eat that," it's gone, gone, gone.

THE ANNOUNCER: The announcer wouldn't dream of leaving the table without feeling confident that everyone knows exactly where he's going, what precisely he'll be doing, how strongly he feels about it and how urgently he needs to be doing it. Does he actually think telling us about his gas pains will encourage our appetites? Before the meal is over, everyone at the table will know that the announcer is lactose intolerant, that he sometimes takes his shoes off under the table and that he may have to leave early because his dog's having a tooth pulled today. Too bad he's deaf to the rest of the table's announcement of "too much information."

BETTY THE CROCKPOT: Betty is the last person you want to be dining out with. Whether it's a $2.00 egg salad from the vending machine or a $40.00 steak, Betty can "bake it better." Nothing is ever satisfactory, and you may as well just throw the menu out the window because she's going to ask for 20 substitutions anyway. It always takes her an hour to decide what she wants, and you know she'll be sending it back anyway when she sees how much better your meal looks. Don't look now; she's headed for the kitchen to give the chef some pointers.

Hmm, I suppose it's good... if you like that sort of thing.

B. Soup it up: Logistics of the lethal liquid

While the question of whether to use a fork or a spoon may not arise, there are many politeness pitfalls to the eating (drinking?) of soup. The potential for slurping, splattering, or slopping is always there. Fortunately, etiquette rules provide a sure-fire solution to your soup woes, and help ensure that all can enjoy their meals in quiet and comfort.

The proper way to eat soup is to take the spoon in hand and keep it sideways. The bowl of the spoon is held parallel to your lips. Gently sweep the spoon in an "away from you" motion over the top of the soup. Let the bottom of the soupspoon brush the outside lip of the soup bowl so that any soup caught on the bottom of the spoon will fall back into the bowl and not end up on your lap or the table linen. Bring the spoon to your mouth. Bending from the waist, your mouth should meet the spoon halfway and both your hand and head should be over the table. Pour the soup sideways into your mouth, being careful not to slurp. It is fine for the spoon to rest on your lips but there is really no need for it to touch your teeth.

Unless you are under the age of five or sick at home in your pajamas eating mom's chicken noodle, it is not appropriate to tear open cellophane wrapped crackers and crunch them into your soup. Crackers are actually intended to be eaten like a biscuit, and don't forget to hold them over your plate as you eat them. There is good news, however. If you wish to sop up soup with your bun, it is okay to do so. The proper way is to tear off bite-sized pieces, drop them in your soup and retrieve them with your spoon rather than your fingers. You may also be happy to know that it is perfectly acceptable to cut the broccoli trees you may find in wonton soups, or long noodles, or the cheese on Swiss onion soup with your knife. This leaves manageable pieces that will fit on your spoon and not splatter your face.

Finally, if you reach the bottom of the bowl and you want to get the last tasty bit, use the plate underneath to tip the bowl slightly away from you and continue with the "out to sea-back to shore" action with the spoon. When you have completed your soup, place the spoon on the plate underneath.

C. Captain of the ship: How to navigate the buffet

No matter where you are on the corporate or social ladder, or how many power lunches and business receptions you've mastered (with the help of Book Two in this series, P's & Q's for Profit), a new business dining dilemma awaits you. The buffet. More and more often tight schedules dictate that the two-hour lunch is a thing of the past. Conveniently, many establishments are bringing back the buffet. Buffets are actually perfect if time is in short supply and/or clients and dining partners will be arriving and leaving at different times. As diversity and individualism become more and more a part of modern business cultures, many corporate planners are suggesting buffets as well for celebrations and business banquets. There's something for everyone; vegetarians, dieters and the hungry, hungry, three-helping types can all get satisfaction. Buffets are also a low-pressure way to encourage mixing and mingling in situations where all the guests don't know each other. Benefits aside, there are rules for navigating the buffet. Pay attention or you'll be sent to the back of the line.

■ **Walk the plank.** When you visit a dining establishment for the purpose of business, remember that business is the priority. The food should be secondary. Choose items you are comfortable eating and avoid having to ask service people a million questions. If you've chosen the buffet, what you see is what you get. It's rude to ask the chef to scrape the onions off your perogies or find you some tomato sauce because you don't like the Alfredo. If you are a fussy eater or you are not easy to please, order a la carte off the menu.

OK, I'll try the house pasta.

■ **Swim with the tide.** It is good manners to let guests know what the agenda is for the meal. Will there be grace? Will there be a guest speaker? Will everyone eat first and talk business later or get the business out of the way before dining? When time is of the essence, agendas are essential.

■ **Eat what you catch.** It's very bad manners to heap your plate and then leave most of it. Take small portions and go back for seconds after everyone else has had a chance to go through the buffet line at least once.

■ **Don't put the little ones back.** Do not eat off of your plate as you progress through the buffet line or nibble off of the food trays as you pass. Don't double dip in dressings or sauces—always use the serving utensils that are provided. Move through the line quickly, so that others behind you can take their turn.

■ **Bait should not be tackled.** If you find you have a food item on your plate which is not tender enough, has difficult bones in it, or is just difficult to handle, set it aside. Don't fight with your food in front of guests or clients, and there is no need to comment aloud on the problem.

■ **Bury your treasure.** Use your napkin! Try to keep the bits of gristle, bones or pieces of chewed beef out of view of your neighbor. Hide the morsels between the folds of your napkin or place them discreetly on your side plate.

D. Taking manners into your own hands: Finger foods

Chances are, in your climb to the top, you've already learned that image is everything. So when you are attending a business or social reception you may choose not to focus on the food at all, thus avoiding any possible messy situation. This may be difficult because it seems that no matter where you go in the business and social world, they'll be tempting you with finger foods and it's hard to be "on" when you're fainting from hunger. Just in case you should you find yourself too busy to nosh before the reception, here are some tips for eating the following standard cocktail foods without making a total mess of yourself:

- **Dainties:** Always take the small paper cup that the cut piece of cake or tart is served with and have an extra napkin on hand. If you have a side plate, use it. Don't pop the whole piece in your mouth at once; try to get at least two bites out of it and don't take more than two pieces at a time.

- **Cheese and pickles:** Use the serving utensil which is provided to take a few pieces and place them on your side plate or napkin. If portions are on toothpicks, leave the toothpick in your napkin; don't put it back onto the serving plate. If you have to slice off cheese, cut small portions and bring them to your plate before taking them to your mouth. When you find pits in olives, discreetly take the pit from your mouth with your fingers and put it in your napkin.

- **Finger sandwiches:** Who can resist these tempting little morsels? Take two or three sandwiches with the tongs which are provided and put them on your plate. Eat each sandwich in at least two or three bites and wipe your hands on a napkin.

- **Vegetables and dips:** Always use a plate or napkin. Use the serving utensils to put a few pieces of vegetables on your plate, and then use the spoon in the dip to put a little dip on your plate. Dip vegetables as you eat them and take manageable bites. Whatever you do, don't double dip into the main dip bowl. If no spoon is provided, ask for one.

- **Hot appetizers:** Take a couple of pieces and place them on your plate; if no plate is provided double up on napkins and use them as a plate. With chicken wings, don't put the whole chicken wing in your mouth and slurp off the meat, instead, hold the wing by the bone and bite off the meat. This is one situation where you may have to leave a little behind. With a skewer, if you are able, hold it sideways in one hand and bite off the meat or vegetables. Again you may have to leave some on the stick and try to resist pointing the skewer towards your throat and ripping the meat off. You may even try breaking the skewer in half, allowing easier access to more of its contents and less chance of sauce on both cheeks.

E. Please don't make me choose the wine!

Unfortunately wine, like etiquette, has gotten a bad rap. People often think that the enjoyment of wine is reserved for the well-educated or well-traveled and that less discriminating types should leave the ordering and tasting to the experts. Not true! There are, of course, many, many wonderful traditions and purposeful protocols when it comes to being a wine connoisseur. It can be very enjoyable to listen to someone in the know tell interesting stories about the geographic details, processes and history of wine. However, when it comes to making people comfortable, the basics of wine etiquette are not really that complicated. Here are some things you may or may not know as well as some basic guidelines:

1. Typically, whoever did the inviting is also doing the paying so that person will also be expected to choose and taste the wine. If you are not comfortable in this role, simply delegate the responsibility to someone who is, either one of the guests who is present or the serviceperson.

2. Despite what most people think, the most expensive wine is not always the best wine. Choose a wine that fits your budget. Regardless of how fantastic a particular vintage is, you will not enjoy it if all you can think about is how much it's costing you.

3. These days there are so many blends and varieties of wine that the old adage of "white wine with white meat " and "red wine with red meat" does not necessarily apply. If you don't have a preference, ask the serviceperson to suggest a wine that compliments your meals or just go ahead and order whatever the majority prefers.

4. If you are a novice wine taster don't be too concerned about knowing all the steps of formal wine tasting. If you've ever had spoiled wine for example, you'll know that it does not take a genius to recognize that the wine is off. It's usually obvious by looking at the portion that has been poured into

your glass and taking a whiff. Unrecognizable "floaters" or cloudiness and a not so pleasant odor are pretty good indicators that you won't be wanting to drink it.

5. When the serviceperson brings the wine to the table, you will be shown the sealed bottle to verify that it is indeed what you ordered. Do check; many an embarrassing moment has arisen at billing time when the host discovers that he just drank two bottles of 1968 Merlot at $275.00 a bottle when he actually wanted the 1986 Merlot at $43.00 a bottle.

6. Sniffing the cork isn't necessary. Typically you are meant to smell the cork and check it for moisture. This is an indication of whether the wine has been stored and aged properly. However, there is really no need to pass the cork around the table, and if you do not have an experienced "wine nose," it is really a waste of time to smell it. Just set it aside and resist the urge to shred it into small pieces or play with it as the dinner progresses.

7. Trust your server. The server will usually pour a small portion of wine into your glass for you to taste. After you or someone of your choosing tastes the wine and nods approval, the server will then pour everyone at the table a small portion and then come back to "top off" the glasses when everyone who is drinking wine has some in their glass. Normally servers won't pour more than a third of a glass of red wine or more than a half a glass of white wine so don't panic if your glass is not filled to the brim. Also note that most restaurants will not serve a wine bucket except with champagne so if you want one, you may have to ask. And, sometimes a server will set a bottle of red wine aside to "breathe" or decant for a short time and then they will return to pour it for you.

8. If you wish to decline a glass of wine don't turn your glass upside down or put your hand over it as the server comes to pour. Simply make eye contact and say, "No thank you," or "I won't be having wine this evening." There is no need to explain to everyone at the table how the nitrates in red wine

give you excruciating headaches or how you had too much last night and need a night off or how you feel strongly that liquor is the devil's nectar. Just say no! If you are the host don't ask people why they are not drinking and don't continue to pour if someone has obviously had enough.

Wine should not be intimidating, especially once you know the basics. But, if you do decide to go a little further in your research and become an expert, remember that it's incredibly rude to make others uncomfortable just because you may know a little more about something than they do. Be careful. You don't want to become like this character:

> **PEDANTIC PAUL:** We've all met him, you know the "I know everything about grapes" wine guy. Pedantic Paul doesn't hesitate to monopolize the conversation and it's hard to resist giggling when he goes on for 20 minutes about the "sentimental bouquet, hints of sun-drenched apple blossoms and witty but not overbearing flavor" of your $7.00 bottle of table wine. Will someone please get him to shut up? You can imagine the show he'll put on when it's time to actually taste the wine. Pass the margaritas instead—who can bear another minute of it?

F. Don't burn the toast

Friends, Romans, Countrymen…lend me your ears. You may not know it yet, but as you climb the ranks you will often be called upon to lead meetings and introduce guests or act as the entertainer and master of ceremonies at many a rubber chicken dinner. Yes, this means the dreaded public-speaking thing. If it's all you can do to get your point across in one-on-one meetings and you shudder at the idea of being in the spotlight, you'd better dry off those sweaty palms and brush up on your podium protocol.

Believe it or not, even polished, experienced speakers have been known to give a bad speech. Some people refer to this as not "being on" but it's really more about not being prepared. When it comes to public speaking, nothing is more important than exuding confidence. Do your research, don't try too hard to be the funny guy or gal if it's just not in you, and speak from the heart. Stick to what you know, stay calm and you'll be okay. Rehearse a little and make sure you don't come off as one of these party poopers!

And then my mother-in-law said...

PETER NO POINTER: Don't look at me I have no idea what he's talking about either. Why do they always choose guys like this to toast the guest of honor? Someone tell a joke—anyone but Peter, he's not so quick with the punch line. Guess we should have stocked up before the bar closed, it's going to be a long night!

MR. MONOTONOUS: Ho hum! It's pretty hard to remain attentive when this dull and boring person talks. Remember the waah, waah, waah thing from Charlie Brown? Tone of voice is often pretty indicative of the speaker's mood or attitude and this guy is almost dead. Someone tell a joke!

And what are the guidelines for toasting? Here are some tips:

- It's not necessary to ferociously clank glasses with everyone at the table. Rumor has it that clanking comes from a very old medieval tradition of purposely hitting your drinking vessel against that of your neighbor hoping that if he put poison in your glass, some would surely spill back into his glass and his hesitating to drink would save you from a quick death.

- It is most appropriate to wait until the main course has been served before you start toasting. This helps ensure that the guests are focused on the presentation rather than a growling or too full stomach.

- You should refrain from jumping up and making toasts unless the host or master of ceremonies has asked you to do so. Most of us can recall a situation where someone who may have had one too many offers a toast at an inopportune time and steals the thunder from someone who was up all night preparing the perfect toast.

- If the toast is to you, remain in your seat and do not drink to yourself. Don't clap either! When the toast is completed, you should rise and respond to the toast, either by offering a toast to someone else or giving a brief statement of thanks.

Remember, as you rise through the ranks, you'll be expected to do more and more public speaking both in business and social situations. You may as well get ready for toasting and hope one day, they're toasting you!

G. Chapter summary

A polished professional understands that a working knowledge of what constitutes appropriate conduct in every social and business situation is mandatory in today's competitive business world. Such knowledge allows one to exhibit confidence, maintain his or her self-respect and build a productive reputation regardless of the scenario. Knowing the technical aspects of good dining manners will allow you to concentrate on the business at hand and exude polish and confidence. Good manners and an ability to communicate an attitude of respect and consideration for others are just good business. Put plain and simply, good business and good manners go hand in hand.

Answers to self-assessment:

1. **c)** All personal belongings should be placed under the chair or table.

2. **c)** You should always greet the guest at the door of the restaurant; treat them as though they were guests in your home.

3. **a)** Arrive on time. There is no such thing as fashionably late and it's impolite to be too early.

4. **c)** Leave the utensil on the floor unless it is dangerous to someone else and discreetly ask the server for another.

5. **b)** Always pass counter clockwise or to your right.

6. **c)** Bring your problem to the attention of the manager.

7. **c)** Don't eat anything that will make you sick. Discreetly have the item removed and another brought.

8. **c)** The napkin goes to the left of the plate.

9. **b)** Utensils are generally used from the outside in.

10. **c)** Never butter the whole bun or whole half at once. Tear or cut in half, tear off bite-sized portions, and butter each portion as you eat it.

Conclusion:
Who gets promoted? You!

Rudeness costs in business! It costs us personally, affecting our relationships, our self-esteem and our reputations; and it costs us professionally, affecting our company's image, our productivity and the bottom line. It doesn't cost much to remember your "please and thank you's," just a little time and consideration. And that small investment has huge returns. Whether we choose to realize it or not, behaviors like showing up late, dressing inappropriately, talking about the wrong thing, being unprepared and behaving like a social buffoon are RUDE! We owe others and ourselves the respect of knowing how to behave. And we need to follow through on that knowledge. Success in business means keeping clients, increasing profits and advancing our careers, all of which is more likely to be accomplished if we can handle ourselves effectively in every possible situation. The client may not remember that you knew exactly what fork to use or that your tie matched your socks, but they will remember that you were confident, prepared and in control—and that's what the boss will remember too when it comes time to decide who gets the promotion!

Acknowledgements:

Building a new business takes strength and perseverance, especially in the first few years. The "beginning" of In Good Company has been a tremendous experience due in part to the ongoing support and positive feedback of many friends and associates. The Etiquette Ladies would like to express heartfelt thanks to Wayne Hrab, Brenda Flemming, Sandy Bergman and Jay Onrait for their continuous encouragement, efforts and assurance.